Money doesn't grow on trees

Jeremy Strong

Adam and Charles Black · London

The Crackers Series

The Custard Kid	Terry Deary
Calamity Kate	Terry Deary
Trouble with Animals	Jeremy Strong
The Lambton Worm	Terry Deary
Lightning Lucy	Jeremy Strong
Fatbag	Jeremy Strong
The Wishing Well Ghost	Terry Deary
The Woff	Jeremy Strong
Money doesn't grow on Trees	Jeremy Strong

Strong, Jeremy
Money doesn't grow on trees.—(The crackers series)
I. Title II. Series
823'.914[J] PZ7

ISBN 0-7136-2400-0

Published by A & C Black (Publishers) Limited
35 Bedford Row, London WC1R 4JH

The illustrations are by Toni Goffe

First published 1984

ISBN 0 7136 2400 0

Filmset by August Filmsetting, Warrington, Cheshire
Printed by R. J. Acford, Chichester, Sussex

1

'You see,' explained Mick to his friend Simon, 'if I had a lot of money I wouldn't worry so much. I spend all my time worrying and it's all because I haven't enough money. So I have to wash the car for 40p and mow the lawn for 50p and do this and do that. I mean, it's slave labour.'

Simon laughed and said nothing. Mick leant back against the shed wall. 'It's all very well for you to laugh,' sulked Mick. 'Your dad gives you three times as much pocket-money as I get, and you don't have to do anything for it. I'm just a slave, a worried slave. I'll probably die of worry. Imagine that! The newspapers would be full of the story:

Nine Year Old Dies of Worry,
Parents Didn't Give Him Enough Money.'

Mick snorted and kicked back against the shed.

'Well how much have you got at the moment?' asked Simon helpfully.

'11p,' said Mick. 'But I owe Mum 52p of that.'

'That's stupid,' said Simon. 'How can you owe 52p when you've only got 11p?'

'Because I broke one of Mum's tea-mugs and she says I've got to pay for another.' Mick sighed. 'I tell you Simon, you don't know what it's like living in my house. Everything I do seems to cost me money. I can't keep up. I'm losing pounds and pounds what with all this worry and slave labour.'

Simon grinned, because Mick was hardly the thinnest boy in the world.

'You can afford to lose some weight,' suggested Simon. Mick was aghast.

'What! You must be joking. Listen, you know what a camel looks like? It's got a great big hump on its back but nobody goes around telling the camel it's fat or ugly or got a hump on its back do they? That's because the camel's hump is useful. The same goes for me – all this fat is for a good purpose.'

Simon glanced down at Mick's bulging tummy and looked rather puzzled.

'Suppose I get stuck in a desert one day,' Mick went on. 'I shall be able to last for days without food, feeding off my own personal hump.'

'But you're not in a desert,' Simon pointed out. 'We're not even anywhere near a desert.'

'Maybe we're not at the moment, but supposing we got suddenly kidnapped and flown out to the middle of the Sahara or the Gobi? Where would you be then? You'd die of starvation within a few hours.' Mick patted his stomach.

'No, this bulge is going to be very useful one day.'

Mick was not only a worrier. He was also a non-stop dreamer. He always had the most marvellous ideas. He could suddenly think up the wildest things. The only problem was that he could never do it at the right time. For example, if they were asked to write stories at school Mick would sit there with his pencil stuck in his mouth and he'd stare blankly out of the classroom window. His head would be full of charging rhinoceroses; deep-sea divers with their feet gripped by giant clams; parachuting soldiers on a secret mission at dead of night; but there would be nothing actually on his piece of paper.

On the other hand Simon could write pages and pages. But the stories that Simon wrote down were never half as good as the ones Mick made up out of thin air when they were playing together, or just talking. Simon shuffled his feet.

'Why don't you make a list of all the money you owe and all the money you can get? Then you can get more money by doing different jobs and gradually cross off what you owe.'

'You mean I've got to write something down?' asked Mick suspiciously.

'Only a little. Get a pencil and a piece of paper and I'll show you.'

Mick nipped indoors. He didn't mind getting the paper if Simon was going to do it for him. He soon came out of the house. 'Here,' he said.

'Right. This is what you do. Put down three columns like this.' Simon carefully divided the scrap of paper into three columns. 'Now you put a heading at the top of each one. Here's the first, GOT. That's what you've got at the moment.'

'I'd never have guessed,' said Mick coldly.

'Look, do you want me to show you or not?'

'Go on, go on,' said Mick with a grin. 'You must realise that this is the most wonderful moment in my life.' Simon kicked him playfully.

'This is the second column, WHAT I OWE.' Mick screwed up his eyes and beat a chubby fist upon his head.

'Don't tell me, don't tell me – that's for the money I owe!' Simon jumped up and down and patted Mick on the back.

'Well done! Michael Shaw, you have won first prize in our Idiot of the Year contest!' Mick fluttered his eyelashes and pressed his hands together in mock delight.

'Oh thank you, thank you. I'm so overwhelmed, I think I shall faint. What's the first prize?' For a moment Simon was stuck. He had to think really hard.

'The first prize,' he announced, 'will be a week's holiday for one person at the South Pole.'

'Lovely,' said Mick. 'I can live off my hump. Come on, tell me what I put in the third column.'

'That's for all the jobs you can do to earn money. You can cross them off as you do them and see how much money you can get.' Mick eyed the grubby piece of paper thoughtfully. He took the pencil from Simon.

'All right,' he said, and he carefully filled in each column so that it looked like this.

'That's all I can think of,' said Mick at last. Simon peered over his shoulder.

'Great! That's £1.80 you can pick up in next to no time.'

'£1.60,' corrected Mick. Simon wasn't very good at maths.

'All right, £1.60. That's a lot of money.'

'It's a lot of work,' grunted Mick. 'Still, I take your point, old genius.'

'It will save a lot of worry having it all written down,' Simon added. 'Any way, I must go or Mum will slaughter me. See you tomorrow, moneybags!'

'Ha ha,' said Mick. 'See you tomorrow.'

Certainly it was a lovely idea to have all that money. There were only two things that spoilt it. The first was that he owed Mum 52p of it and the second was all the work involved. Mind you, he already had 11p to start with so that made £1.71 minus the 52p he owed Mum. That left him with . . . Mick scratched his head. Well, it left him with less than £1.71. If he was going to keep his hump supplied he'd have to start work right away.

Mick went back outside and looked at the lawn. He imagined himself pushing the rusty lawnmower up and down, up and down. Dad would insist on having straight lines. Maybe he could tow the mower behind his bike? He went out to the front of the house and looked at Dad's car. He'd have to wash it, then dry it, then put the polish on, then rub the polish off . . . Mick clapped one hand over his eyes, he couldn't bear the thought. He imagined himself blinded for life by the dazzling glare of the car he'd just polished. He heaved a long sigh and trudged into the garage to fetch a bucket.

The first bit was easy. All he had to do was slosh

water all over the car and give it a quick rub-down with the sponge. Mick usually enjoyed that bit. He filled the bucket with cold water and stood to one side of the car. Then he aimed the bucket at the car and threw the lot in one big splash. It was supposed to splash, but it didn't. The water simply disappeared. Mick stepped forwards with a puzzled frown.

A small trickle of water dripped from the bottom of one front door and Mick noticed with a dreadful pang that the car's side-windows were wide open. The water had gone straight through the window and was now swirling about the floor of the car and dribbling off the front seats.

Mick hurriedly covered the open window with his back and looked over at the house to see if anybody had noticed. Dad didn't come out waving an axe or spraying bullets from a shoulder-slung machine gun so Mick decided that so far he was in the clear. He reached behind and carefully opened one front door just a crack. A stream of icy water poured over the edge of the car and soaked the back of Mick's trousers, filling up his shoes at the same time. Mick shut his eyes and groaned softly. Then he squelched into the garage to find a cloth to mop up the car before anybody found out.

The cloth he found wasn't terribly clean, but since it was the only one, there was nothing Mick could do about it. He couldn't very well ask Mum for a cloth. She'd ask him what it was for and then what could he say? Cleaning his bike? He hadn't cleaned his bike for three years. Polishing his guitar? He didn't have a guitar. No, it was pointless. He would have to make do with what he had.

Mick tiptoed out to the car and opened the door that was furthest away from the house. Another stream of water trickled out from this side but Mick was ready for it and smiled to himself. He reached into the car and began to wipe the dribbles of water from the seats.

It was some time before Mick realised that although he was drying the seats they were covered with curious grey smudges. He carried on for a few more seconds and then discovered with horror that the grey smudges were coming off the cloth he was using. It was oil. Mick straightened up and threw the cloth on the ground. What was the point? He might as well give himself up now. Whatever he did now was bound to make matters even worse. It always did. Mick slowly walked over to the house and went in, thinking to himself.

What would Dad do? Was it against the law for fathers to strangle their own children? Perhaps Dad would burn his body to get rid of the evidence. Perhaps Dad would turn him into this year's Guy Fawkes. Maybe he ought to run away and escape a terrible fate.

Too late. Dad was just coming down the stairs. 'That was quick, Mick. Have you finished?' Mick mumbled an answer and shook his head at the same time. Dad was already feeling in his pocket for some money to pay his son.

'You get quicker every time,' said Dad amiably. 'Let's go and have a look.'

Mick coughed on his words. 'Dad,' he spluttered. 'Um, I don't think, the trouble is, and, well, oil you see, I didn't . . .'

'What are you mumbling about?' asked Dad. Mick sighed.

'I've boobed,' he said simply. Dad's head began to nod up and down very slowly. Mick thought he looked like one of those tiny plastic animals you often see in the back of cars. They have heads on springs and bounce up and down as the car travels along. Mick wished for an instant that his dad actually was one of those tiny animals – boyoing, boyoing . . .

'Mick,' said Dad, 'how have you boobed?' As an answer to this question of questions Mick led the way outside.

Dad stood looking at the car from the front garden. 'I don't see anything wrong.' Still without saying a word Mick opened the driver's door. Dad came round to the side of the car and peered in. He started nodding again. Without thinking Mick found his own head going up and down in sympathy with his dad's. He clapped one hand on top of his head.

'What is it?' asked Dad. Mick wondered if Dad was talking about the oil or the water.

'Water,' said Mick.

'Water? That's more like oil. What water? I can't see any . . . oh! That water! Mick, where is your brain?' Dad turned on his son. 'I've told you before to check all the windows first. You've soaked the inside of the car.' Dad bent down and picked up the cloth Mick had used for drying up.

'I suppose you used this to dry the seats?' Mick nodded. 'It's got oil on it,' said Dad. 'Didn't you see it had oil on it?' Mick shook his head.

'Why didn't you ask your mother for a clean cloth?' demanded his father.

Mick shrugged his shoulders and looked dismally up at his father. 'Because I haven't got a guitar,' he said hoarsely, and winced at his own foolishness. Dad threw up his hands.

'What do you mean you haven't got a guitar? What's that got to do with putting oil stains all over my car seats? Are you mad? Listen, it will take a lot of hard rubbing to get that oil off. I shall have to buy special oil stain remover for that. Do you know how much it costs? About £1.50 a bottle. £1.50! Who's going to pay for it, that's what I'd like to know. Money doesn't grow on trees you know.' Dad stopped for a few seconds to get his breath back.

'You're going to pay for that oil stain remover, Mick, all right? You can pay me half the cost.

That's 75p you owe me and I'll have it at the weekend. Now for goodness sake scram, and keep away from my car.'

Mick hurried into the house and went straight upstairs to his bedroom. He threw himself onto the bed and his weight made the bed creak painfully. Mick lay on his back with his hands clasped under his head. He stared up at the ceiling. He stayed staring at the ceiling for a long time. At last he reached into his pocket and pulled out the crumpled piece of paper that Simon had written on. He got a pencil and made a few additions. He crossed out 'Wash car 40p'. He wrote 75p under the 52p in the WHAT I OWE column. That made £1.27 he owed and he hadn't earned any money at all.

Mick decided that perhaps it would have been better to have been burnt as Guy Fawkes after all.

2

The first thing Mick saw when he got up the following morning was a tatty, crumpled piece of paper, lying on his clothes chest. WHAT I OWE, he read glumly. He shoved his feet hard into his shoes. £1.27, he thought. That's what I owe. His shoes seemed very cold and clammy. Looking down, Mick discovered that he'd forgotten to put on any socks. He opened a drawer and swirled his hand round amongst the clothes. What did it matter? Mum would only have to wash them if he wore any. Mick bent down and tied his laces. For some strange reason, wearing shoes with no socks made him feel like an explorer deep in the jungle, his ears filled with the staccato chatter of monkeys and the furious trumpeting of rogue elephants.

'Mick!'

Hold it, thought Mick carefully. I don't remember telling any elephants my name.

'Mick! Breakfast! Get a move on.' It was Mum. Mick plodded downstairs, carefully stepping over the sleeping python stretched across the hallway.

Mick plopped down on a seat in the tiny kitchen and began to eat the bacon and eggs that Mum had cooked for him. Mum stood back and watched him.

'Tell me, why aren't you wearing any socks?' asked Mum. Mick hurriedly tried to finish his mouthful of food before answering.

'It's to save you washing,' he said.

'That's very thoughtful of you, Mick, but really I don't mind washing your socks.' Mick shoved several chips in his mouth.

'I thought,' he continued, chewing at the same time, 'I thought that if I didn't wear any socks it would save at least 52p's worth of washing powder. Probably a lot more. In fact,' Mick went on, getting quite worked up by the idea that had just occurred to him, 'if you didn't wash any of my socks for a week you'd end up owing me money.' Mick glanced up at Mum's raised eyebrows. 'Probably,' he added hastily.

'I doubt it very much,' said Mum.

'It was only an idea,' said Mick.

'Good. Don't bother to try it. Please put some socks on. I don't want you going out on the streets looking like some jungle explorer.'

Mick went back upstairs to get some socks. The python had moved and been replaced by a rather ferocious crocodile. Mick spent several minutes wrestling with it underwater. He only stopped when Mum told him to. While he was upstairs he pocketed the list and then decided to wander over to Simon's house.

Simon did not live very far from Mick, and Mick usually visited Simon's place rather than the other way round. This was because the Shaws were very proud of their house and garden. Everything was neat and tidy and well kept. There were no weeds or untidy verges. Passers-by often remarked how beautifully kept the garden was. This was quite true, but as Mick would quickly point out, a beautiful garden isn't much fun, unless you happen to like beautiful gardens.

Simon's garden kept making a brave attempt to be lovely but it was always defeated by Simon and Mick. They used the garden as a football-pitch, running track, cattle-ranch and inter-stellar battlestation.

'Hey!' cried Simon, as soon as Mick appeared. 'Guess what my dad brought home last night?' He was obviously wildly pleased with whatever it was. Mick hated these moments. Simon's dad was always bringing home strange things. It didn't seem to matter whether they were small or large, they were always interesting. Once Simon's dad brought home an old electric motor off a sewing machine. It still worked and Simon and his dad tried to make it drive an old toy lorry until the engine broke under the strain. Another time he had brought back an enormous cardboard box which had had a freezer unit inside it. It was just a giant-sized box but Simon and Mick had used it for days and days before they left it out in the rain one night and it had turned from a box into a soggy cardboard pudding.

The only thing that Mick's dad ever brought home were pretty little plants in little wooden trays to be planted out in the garden. And here was Simon with yet another something. What was it this time? Mick walked up the path while Simon dashed back into the house. A moment later he emerged, carrying what looked like a very slim vacuum cleaner. Simon held it out for Mick to see. Mick whistled. It was a metal detector.

'Here, I'll show you how it works,' said Simon. He pressed a pair of earphones over Mick's head and handed him the handle of the machine. Simon switched it on and Mick immediately heard a slow crackle in his ears. He moved the flat disc at the bottom of the handle across the ground and soon the crackles rose into a whine.

'I've got something!' cried Mick. He peered down at the ground.

'It's a nail,' said Simon, picking it up. 'Rusty too.'

'This is fantastic,' said Mick, pulling off the earphones.

'I know. We can use it whenever we like, Dad says, so long as we're careful. We could go out in the garden and see if we can find any coins on the ground, amongst the long grass.' Mick brightened.

'We might find a whole hoard of coins,' dreamed Mick.

'Not very likely.'

'Why not? You don't know what happened here before your house was built, do you? Suppose there was a robbery on the main road two hundred years ago, and the escaping highwayman decided to bury his treasure right here.' Mick stamped on the ground beneath his feet.

'Supposing he didn't?' asked Simon. 'Supposing he buried it over there? Then we'll have dug over here for nothing, won't we?'

Mick waved the metal-detector. 'Not with this. This will tell us exactly where to dig. Come on, I could do with some extra money. I owe £1.27 at the moment.'

'£1.27,' cried Simon. 'I thought it was only 52p?'

'Yes, well it's a long story.' Mick rammed the headphones over his curly hair and began to wander across Simon's front garden, pushing the disc of the machine this way and that. He listened raptly to the crackle in his ears. It began to whine and Mick held the machine steadily over the source of the whine.

'There's something here,' he cried excitedly.

'Grass,' replied Simon. 'All right, hold your horses, I'll have a look.' Simon peered beneath the machine but could see nothing.

'It must be underneath,' he said. 'I'll get a trowel.'

'I bet it's treasure,' said Mick. 'I can tell by the whine.'

'Oh, I didn't realise you were an expert in the art of metal detecting,' said Simon sarcastically. 'Honestly, you find a rusty nail and think you're marvellous.' He stumped off and fetched a trowel. Then he carefully began to dig up the lawn, piling up the earth next to the hole he was making.

'Come on,' said Mick impatiently. Simon straightened up.

'Found it,' he said stonily.

'What is it?'

Simon was holding up a shapeless twist of metal, no larger than a bar of chocolate.

'Well it must be metal or the machine wouldn't have whined.'

'It's not much use though is it?' said Mick, switching the machine back on.

The search went on. Gradually more and more holes appeared over the garden, each with its little pile of earth next to it. The two boys found more nails, a knife without a handle, part of an old toy and an old tea-caddy, covered with mud and rust. This last provoked great excitement.

'Somebody must have buried it,' exclaimed Mick. 'Nobody goes around putting tea-caddies in their garden unless they are burying something on purpose.'

'Perhaps they just didn't like the tea in it,' suggested Simon. 'If they'd been given some awful tea by an aunt or something for Christmas they might have buried it to get rid of it.'

'People don't bury tea,' insisted Mick. 'Here, let me open it.' He snatched the caddy from Simon who had been unable to prise the lid open.

'Well, what do people bury?' demanded Simon.

'Money of course, stolen money.' At that moment the lid flew open and the contents of the tea caddy were revealed. There was nothing in the tin except for a huddle of tiny, dried-out bones. The boys stared down at them and slowly looked up at each other.

'Of course,' said Mick slowly. 'Sometimes people bury things that have died. What do you think it was?' Simon shook his head.

'Budgie? or maybe it was a hamster or a guinea-pig.' Mick carefully closed the lid. He pushed the caddy gently back into the ground and the boys swept the disturbed earth back over the tea-caddy-coffin.

'Some treasure,' muttered Simon. He picked up the detector and began another tour of the grass.

Simon's mother, Mrs Crane, came back from her shopping. She plonked her heavy bags down on the path and eyed the holes all over her front garden.

'What's going on here then?' she asked. 'Let's all go to Australia week? Or are you building a new golf-course for the area?' She suddenly noticed Simon lurking in the bushes with the metal-detector.

'All right Simon, I can see you.' Simon came out sheepishly. 'The trouble your dad causes, I don't know. This garden looks as if a mole has just had his eighteenth birthday party on it.' Mrs Crane laughed to herself. 'You boys – I'll never get this garden straight until you're grown up.'

She picked up the shopping and went inside. Mick really liked Mrs Crane. She seemed so straightforward. He wished his own mum was like her. He wished his dad was like Mr Crane for that matter. Mick sighed.

'I'd better get home for lunch,' he said.

'O.K. Are you coming back this afternoon?'

'Expect so.' Mick wandered off towards his own house, dragging his feet. One foot kicked something small and metallic. It scurried across the paving stones and pinged against a garden wall. Mick bent down and picked it up. It was a £1 piece. Mick couldn't believe it. He took in a long slow breath that almost burst all his shirt buttons and beamed to himself. He slipped the cold coin into his trouser pocket and marched to his house. £1.00!

As soon as he got home Mick got out the piece of paper and re-adjusted all his columns. It now said:

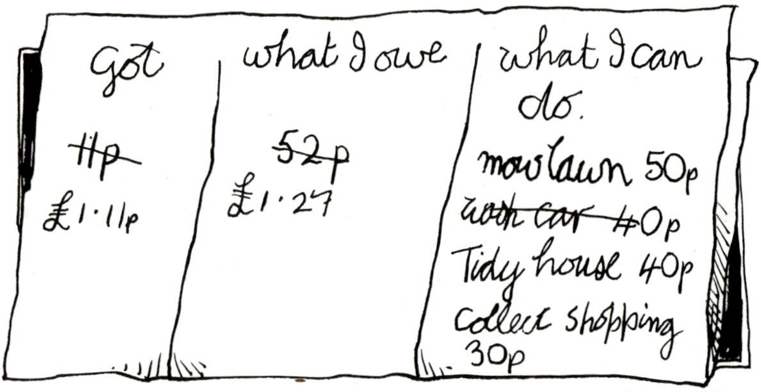

He only needed to get another 16p and he'd be even. He wouldn't owe anybody anything. Mick scanned his list. Tidy house, maybe he should do that next. Maybe he could get Simon to help him while Mrs Shaw was out having her hair done or something.

Normally Mrs Shaw didn't like having Simon in the house because the two of them made twice as much mess as usual. Suddenly Mick found himself wondering yet again why he couldn't have parents like Simon's. Before he finished day-dreaming, his mother came into the house. She looked a bit flustered.

'I am stupid,' she said to her son. 'I only went up the road to give Mrs Carter some plant cuttings and somehow I lost £1 on the way there. It just rolled out of my bag and went. I've searched and searched.' She sat down and wiped her forehead with a small handkerchief.

Mick turned red and then white. He fumbled in his pocket and felt the coin against his stubby fingers. He took a deep breath.

'I just found £1,' he murmured. He held the coin out to his mother.

'But that's it!' cried Mrs Shaw delightedly. 'Well done Mick. How did you know where it was?'

'My foot kicked it and I heard it ping,' said Mick flatly. Mrs Shaw put it carefully into her bag.

'I'm very grateful. That was very clever of you,' said his mum, 'and honest too.' She got up cheerfully and went out to the kitchen. Mick slumped back in his chair, mentally re-arranging his list back to what it was before. He wished that the ceiling would cave in on him, or a suddenly revived tyrannosaurus would poke its massive head through the window and snap him up into oblivion. Or even better, perhaps a tiny radio-controlled aeroplane would come whirring through the window and fly over his head and then drop £1 000 by parachute right into his lap. And there'd be a note wrapped round the bundle of money that said: 'This money is for Michael Shaw *only*.'

'Mick? Mick, do stop dreaming.' Mick sat up with a start. Mum was standing next to his chair. She smiled down at him.

'Look, it was very lucky of you to find that £1. I really am very pleased. I'll tell you what, we'll split it.' Mick blinked. How could you split a £1 piece? He had a sudden vision of his mother wildly swinging an enormous Viking axe and bringing it whamming down upon the little coin.

"You keep 50p and I'll keep 50p,' said Mrs Shaw. She put two 20p coins and a 10p on the arm of Mick's chair. Mick sat forward. He grinned.

'Thanks Mum. Thanks very much.' Life was getting better, perhaps he'd ask the tyrannosaurus to come back another day. Mrs Shaw gave Mick a quick pat on the head.

'That's all right. And I'll tell you what. We'll forget about that 52p for the mug. It would have been very easy for you to have kept quiet about finding that money. I'm glad you told me. It must have been very difficult for you.'

Mick jumped right out of the chair. 'Thanks Mum!' he cried and ran upstairs to re-write his list yet again. Maybe he'd tell the tyrannosaurus not to bother to call back at all.

3

That same afternoon Mick once more considered his list.

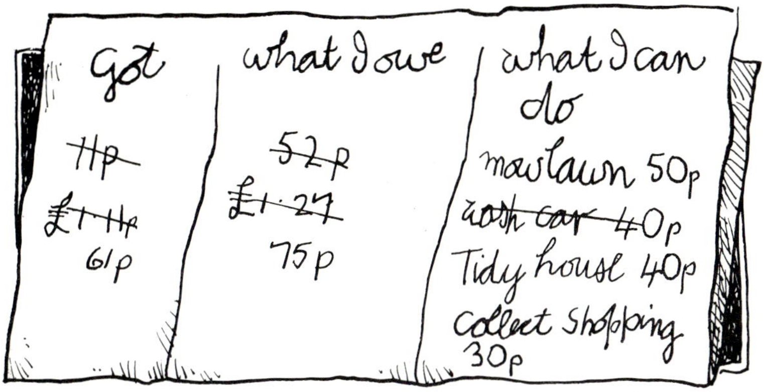

Mick sat back thoughtfully and after a few moments he leant forward and wrote in the 'what I can do' column: Rob Bank £2 000 000. It was an excellent idea, thought Mick. All he had to do was overcome the alarm system, the security guards and the waiting police and then he'd be rich. Mick couldn't think what he would spend £2 000 000 on. Maybe it was a bit much really. He didn't wish to be greedy. He crossed out £2 000 000 and put £1 000 000 instead. Then he sat and wondered how he would set about robbing a bank.

The element of surprise was the most important thing in any robbery. Mick had watched countless television films about bank thefts and always the most important part was the surprise. Nobody must suspect anything. After a few minutes of hard thinking Mick worked out a plan. It was quite simple really. First he would make a trip to the pet-shop where he would buy up the entire stock of mice and rats, gerbils, guinea-pigs and hamsters. He might possibly buy any snakes they had as well, just for good measure. Then he'd go into the bank and release all his animals. The staff would go mad and while they were charging all over the place and quivering with fear, Mick would scoop up all the money.

On second thoughts, maybe this plan wouldn't work too well. Still, at least he only needed 14p now and then he wouldn't owe anybody anything. Mind you, he wouldn't have anything either. Mick got up and wandered over to Simon's. His friend was still combing the lawn with the metal-detector.

'Have you found anything?' Mick asked. Simon took off the headphones and sat down on the garden wall. He nodded.

'What?'

'One old sardine tin, an ant's nest, three milk-bottle tops and five unidentifiable buried objects, or UBOs for short.' Simon pointed at a small pile of dirty, rusty metal.

'We're just looking in the wrong places,' said Mick. 'This garden is no use.'

'Where do you suggest we try?' asked Simon. Mick smiled.

'Well, we could try a bank.'

'Yes,' said Simon, 'that's a very good idea Mick. Let's try a bank and get ourselves arrested.'

'Don't worry,' Mick said. 'I know how to get us out of jail. With the Mick Shaw patent jail-escape mechanism we'd be free in no time.'

'Tell me, O great and fascinating Mick Shaw the Wonderful, what is this superbly exciting Mick Shaw patent jail-escape mechanism?'

'Ah!' said Mick, and he rapidly outlined his marvellous invention. The idea had first occurred to him after watching a television programme about fire-prevention. The programme showed how if you mix some kind of foam with a special chemical, the foam expands very quickly and fills up any large space and smothers the flames. 'So,' said Mick, 'What you do is smuggle in some foam and this special chemical and you pack out the cell window with the stuff and add the chemical. The foam expands and as it does so it either pushes out the bars or even pushes out the whole window. It's perfect!'

Simon considered the idea carefully.

'Well, just one or two points,' he said. 'Suppose you push out the window successfully . . .'

'Yes?'

'And then find you're five floors up?'

'Use your sheets as a parachute,' Mick suggested.

'Or suppose the foam expands into the cell and smothers you.'

'Oh, in that case you'd be dead and wouldn't worry about anything.'

Simon jumped off the wall. 'You're an idiot,' he said cheerfully. 'Come on, let's go and try the fields with the metal-detector.' The fields were only a few streets away and didn't take long to reach. They belonged to a small farm that was now surrounded by houses. The boys climbed over a broken fence into a field of grass that had one, solitary horse in it, slowly chomping away.

'Where do we start?' asked Simon. Mick shrugged his shoulders. Simon pulled the earphones over his head and switched the detector on. He began to sweep the disc over the grass. Mick followed him slowly, idly swishing at the grass with a stick. Supposing they didn't find any money, or any treasure? They might just find a hidden passageway leading to an underground rocket-station where the infamous Colonel Garst was plotting to take over the world. It was just possible, thought Mick, that the slowly chewing horse was Colonel Garst in disguise.

Colonel Garst was a character Mick had invented during a game with Simon, several weeks previously. Since then the boys found themselves quite often fighting against this dreaded secret agent. Mick tapped Simon on the shoulder and hissed at him.

'Don't look now,' he murmured under his breath, 'but I think that horse over there is Colonel Garst.' Simon slowly turned his head to spy on the luckless creature.

'Yikes, you're right! What shall we do?'

'Leave this to me,' whispered Mick. Mick wandered nonchalantly over to the old brown horse, picked up a handful of grass and then ran back to Simon, yelling.

'Get down!' Mick and Simon threw themselves upon the ground, while Mick made the sound of a muffled explosion. He stood up and rubbed his hands.

'What did you do?' asked Simon incredulously.

'Oh, I simply fed him some special explosive grass,' explained Mick. 'It was nothing at all.' Simon pumped his friend's hand.

'You were wonderful, you saved us all. Here, have the Victoria Cross, and the Charing Cross, and Waterloo Station . . .'

'Waterloo Station?' repeated Mick, taking a step back. 'I can't wear that, it's too heavy.'

'Ah!' cried Simon suddenly. 'It's whining, the machine's whining!' The two boys got down on their knees and began to dig furiously.

'Careful,' said Mick, 'It may be valuable.' They cleared away the earth and gradually revealed a long, shapeless, reddish-brown object, heavily encrusted with rust. Simon worked at it until he could pull it out of the ground.

'What do you think it is?' he asked Mick. Mick sucked in his cheeks thoughtfully.

'Difficult to say. I mean, it would be much easier to say what it isn't.'

'How do you mean?' demanded Simon.

'Well, it's not an elephant for example,' said Mick authoritatively. 'I don't think it's a Phantom jet either. Or Buckingham Palace.'

'We're not getting very far,' said Simon. Mick looked round the field.

'We haven't moved at all,' he pointed out, but Simon didn't even see the joke.

Mick took the heavy object from Simon and looked at it more closely.

'It's sort of pointed at one end,' he said. He ran his fingers down the sides.

'You know what it is? It's a sword.'

'Don't be daft,' cried Simon. 'That's never a sword.'

'Listen,' Mick explained. 'It's been in the ground for hundreds of years. It probably got left by some dying soldier. It could be a Cavalier sword, or a Norman sword, or even a Viking sword. It's got covered and covered with layers of rust. It doesn't look like a sword now, but if you cleaned all the rust off I bet you'd find it was one.' Mick balanced the treasure carefully in his hands. 'This is worth a lot of money. It's ancient. They put things like this in museums because they're valuable.'

At that moment Colonel Garst in the disguise of a horse wandered up to the boys and poked his massive brown head between them. The horse snuffled at them.

'I thought you blew him up with explosive grass?' said Simon.

'Idiot! Can't you tell the difference between Colonel Garst and a real horse?'

'Not when you're around,' said Simon. 'How do you tell?'

'You examine the teeth,' confided Mick.

'What are we going to do with the famous sword?' Simon asked.

'Let's take it back home and clean it up.'

They carried the sword home carefully and took it into the garage at Simon's house. Here they found some stiff wire brushes and they set about scrubbing away the dry earth and flakes of rust. Some of the rust broke off but the task was far more difficult than either of the boys had expected.

Mr Crane wandered into the garage. He was a small, wiry man with a cheerful moustached face and dirty check shirt. He bent over the boys and watched them for a minute.

'What have you got there?' he asked.

'A sword,' replied Mick. 'We found it out in the horse field.'

'Could be,' said Mr Crane. 'Mind you it could be anything, that shape.'

'It's got a handle,' Simon pointed out.

'Probably,' said Mr Crane with a smile, and he left them to it.

Ten minutes later they gave up brushing at the rust. They didn't seem to have removed much.

'How much do you think ancient swords are worth?' asked Simon.

'Oh I don't know. About £1 000 I should think, unless it's a prehistoric sword. They're worth millions.'

'They didn't have swords in prehistoric times,' said Simon swiftly.

'That's why they're worth so much,' answered Mick easily. 'Rarity value!'

'How will we find out about this one?'

'We could take it down to the museum and get them to identify it for us. Then they'd pay us and it would go on display in a special glass cabinet and there'd be a label saying *Anglo Saxon Sword Discovered by Michael Shaw and Simon Crane.*

'Don't you think we ought to try and find out about it somewhere else first of all?' suggested Simon. 'I mean, we'd look pretty stupid if it turned out to be a lump of rusted iron and that's all.' Mick was horrified at the thought. He held out the mangled object like a crown on a velvet cushion.

'Look at it!' he cried. 'How can you call it a lump

of rusted iron. Look, it's pointed at one end and knobbly at the other where the handle was.' Mick looked darkly at his friend. 'I shouldn't be surprised,' he went on, 'if the dark stains down both sides don't come from blood.'

'Blood!' cried Simon.

'Anglo-Saxon blood,' repeated Mick.

So it was that they took the sword down to the little museum. The museum was also a library and the lady at the desk didn't take kindly to the entrance of two boys carrying a large lump of rusted metal. She peered over her pink-framed glasses and sniffed.

'Excuse me,' she piped. 'Would you mind taking that bit of old junk out?'

'Bit of old junk!' said Mick. He waved the lump above his head. 'This is an Anglo-Saxon sword and we've come to have it identified,' he explained.

The lady raised her eyebrows slowly and pursed her lips together so that all the blood drained from them. 'Well, if you insist on bringing it in, for goodness sake stop waving it about. You want Mr Ferris in the museum.' She pointed towards a small door at the side of the library section.

'Thanks,' said Mick and they marched over to the door and knocked on it.

'Come in.'

Mr Ferris was extremely large. The boys found him sitting in a revolving chair. At least, Mick thought to himself, he's not sitting in it, he's overflowing in it. Mr Ferris had a large beard full of grey and white and black hairs. It flourished downwards and sideways and was most impressive, but not as impressive as his eyebrows. These were great tufts that stuck out for at least a centimetre and jumped about like dancing caterpillars as he spoke.

'What's that you've got there?' Mr Ferris asked.

'We don't know,' said Simon. 'We thought, we hoped you might be able to tell us. We found it buried in a field and we, at least my friend, thought it might be valuable.' Mr Ferris looked at Mick and smiled.

'So you thought it might be valuable?' Mick nodded. 'How much do you think it's worth?' asked Mr Ferris, and his eyebrows scuttled up his head and then down again.

'I was hoping for about a thousand pounds,' muttered Mick, shifting from one leg to the other. Mr Ferris gave a low whistle.

'A thousand pounds. That's a lot of money. Why do you think it's worth that much?'

'He thinks it's an Anglo-Saxon sword,' interrupted Simon.

'No I don't,' said Mick hotly, suddenly feeling rather foolish, 'that was just a joke.'

Mr Ferris fingered the rusted lump. 'Hmmm. It could be a sword, and then again it might be something else. It's very difficult to tell with all this rust on it.'

'Can you tell how old it is?' asked Mick. Mr Ferris shook his head.

'Not straight away. We'd need to do tests on it first and that costs a fair bit of money.' He looked at the boys. 'You two got much money?'

'I've got minus 14p,' explained Mick. 'That's because I owe my dad 14p.'

Simon just pulled out his empty pockets. Mr Ferris grunted. 'Leave it with me. I'll see what I can do. But don't get too hopeful. It's more than likely that this is just a lump of scrap metal.'

The boys thanked him and hurried home. Mick was thinking. A thousand pounds. You could probably buy a camel for a thousand pounds.

4

Mick decided that things were getting serious. It was all very well to be only 14p in debt but how was he to survive when he still owed money? It was true that eventually the weekend would come and he would receive his pocket-money, but that wouldn't get him very far. Mick carefully placed both hands upon his stomach. He was certain it was shrinking.

Mick wasn't a compulsive eater. He wasn't a bit like Billy Bunter. He wasn't even grossly fat. It was simply that Mick's stomach was a bit larger than most boys' and because it was larger it needed more food to fill it. At least that's the reason Mick gave to anybody who asked. He felt duty bound to make sure his stomach was well looked after. To Mick it was like a National Monument, a stately home that needed constant upkeep to maintain it in good condition.

That thought had never occurred to Mick before and it gave him a good idea. Maybe he could set up a fund for his stomach, a *Save Mick's Stomach* appeal. He could do some kind of sponsored walk . . . no, that would be no use. That would simply make him even thinner. A sponsored feast . . . that could be a good idea. Yet Mick wasn't even too worried about maintaining his tummy. He just wanted more money. He wasn't too sure what he wanted it for but Mick was certain that he had great need for more of it.

Mick wandered through to the kitchen to see if there was anything he could do to earn some. He was a bit fed up with staring at his list and thinking about mowing the lawn or doing the shopping. He couldn't think of anything more boring. His mother was preparing some salad.

'Don't tell me,' said Mum, as soon as Mick wandered in with that certain expression on his face. 'You're going to ask me what you can do to earn some money.'

'How did you know?' asked Mick, genuinely surprised.

'I can see little pound signs whirring round your eyeballs,' Mum said. 'I don't understand why you have this sudden urge to become a millionaire.'

Mick slumped down on one of the kitchen chairs and idly pinched a carrot and began chewing it.

'Just in case,' he said.

'In case of what?'

'Well, it could be anything. Suppose you and Dad suddenly got killed?'

'Thank you very much!' Mum cried. 'It's not very likely.'

'I'm only supposing,' said Mick hastily. 'You asked me. Just supposing a plane passing overhead suddenly develops engine failure and comes crashing down on this house killing all its occupants.'

'What about you?' asked Mum.

'Oh I'm playing over at Simon's when the tragedy occurs. Anyway,' continued Mick, 'there I am with no parents. I'll need money then won't I?'

'But Mick,' said Mum quietly, 'I really don't think this dreadful tragedy is likely to occur.'

'No,' agreed Mick. 'But I ought to be prepared just in case.' He stretched across the table and stole a slice of cucumber. 'Anyway, there must be something I can do to earn some money?' He looked expectantly at Mum.

'I wondered when you'd ask. What about mowing the lawn?' Mick rolled his eyes.

'How about the shopping. There's quite a lot of shopping to get.' Mick drummed his fingers on the table, irritably.

'Isn't there something a bit more interesting that I could do?' he asked.

'What sort of thing?' asked Mum.

'Well . . .' there was a long pause.

'I'll tell you what. You see all this salad stuff I'm making? It costs the earth to buy in the shops. I've been standing here peeling potatoes and looking out of the window. What we ought to do is grow all our own salad stuff. Look at that garden. I know your father has made it look very pretty with flowers and a lovely lawn and everything. But we could easily use a small bit of the bottom end for a vegetable patch and then we can grow our own lettuce and cucumber. It will save us pounds and pounds. Why don't you dig a vegetable patch for me?'

Mick was aghast at the thought. He clutched his throat and with a wild strangulated gurgle he fell to the ground. 'Aaargh,' he choked. 'Dig the garden! I've been killed by the thought!'

'For goodness sake get up and stop being such a clown. It won't take you long.'

'It will take days!' cried Mick, gradually getting up from the floor. 'It will take weeks, months, years. I tell you Mum, you'll look out there in twenty years time and I shall still be toiling away over my spade, bent double with a long grey beard and covered with masses of snow and apples . . .'

Mum could not help laughing. 'How on earth can you be covered in snow and apples?' she asked, wiping her tears of laughter from her eyes with the corner of her apron. 'Honestly Mick, you are such a clown.'

'Look at the three apple trees down there,' Mick

pointed out. 'By the time I've worked beneath those trees for twenty years I'm bound to be covered in apples. They'll probably take root in my beard and I shall have tiny little apple trees sprouting from my beard and cuckoos flying in and out all day long crying cuckoo! cuckoo! just like clocks, and woodpeckers drilling away . . .'

'You're cuckoo if you ask me,' said Mum. 'Now stop your idiotic chatter and listen. If you dig me a good vegetable patch I'll give you two pounds.'

Mick looked at Mum unbelievingly. 'Two pounds?' he repeated. Mum nodded.

'But it will have to be a good patch. I don't want something the size of a tea-towel. I want a decent vegetable garden so that I can grow lettuce and beans and maybe some strawberries.'

'Strawberries? You're going to grow some strawberries?'

'It's possible,' replied Mum.

'And you'll pay me two pounds *and* possibly grow strawberries?'

'Yes.'

'I shall have to consider this very carefully,' said Mick slowly. 'Can I have time to consider this offer?'

'By all means,' said Mum. 'But I shall need it dug within the next two weeks.'

Mick left the kitchen and went outside, making his way slowly over to Simon's house. The idea of earning two whole pounds was very attractive, but Mick knew that there would be a lot of hard work involved, and Mick was not very attracted to hard work. On the other hand he was rather fond of strawberries.

Simon was coming down the road towards Mick's house, so they met half-way. Simon was carrying the metal-detector.

'Have you found anything good yet?' asked Mick.

'Not really. I thought we could try up by the small pond.'

'Which one?' enquired Mick. There were three rather small ponds fairly close by.

'The one halfway up the hill, you know, where all the trees are, where we had that rope swing, only you broke it.'

'I didn't break it!' said Mick. 'The rope was all frayed.'

'It was the extra weight,' continued Simon. 'The rope couldn't take the strain.'

'It was frayed,' Mick insisted. 'All right, let's go up to the pond.' The boys set off up the hill.

'Have you got any money yet?' Simon asked.

'I'm still on minus 14p, but Mum's offered me two pounds if I dig the garden.'

'Two pounds!' exclaimed Simon. 'What are you waiting for?'

'Well hopefully somebody who will do it for me,'

said Mick, grinning. 'Or maybe we could even invent an automatic radio-controlled spade, then I could sit there in a deck-chair sipping at my glass of coke and twiddle a few knobs while the automatic spade does all the work.'

'Why don't you just get on and dig it? It won't take you long,' said Simon.

Mick grunted. 'It's all very well for you to say that. You don't have to do all the work.' He pointed at the pond which they had now reached. 'Where shall we start?'

In answer to this Simon handed over the detector to Mick. 'You have a go,' he said. Mick slipped the head-phones over his head.

'Thanks.' he said. 'Finders keepers?' Simon shrugged his shoulders.

'All right,' he said. 'Finders keepers, but we won't find anything.'

'Don't say that. I've got a sort of strange sensation in my stomach that we're going to find something special today.'

'That reminds me,' said Simon. 'How long do you think it will be before we hear from Mr Ferris about that sword?'

'No idea. He said the sword would have to be sent away so I suppose it will be at least a week. Anyway, I don't suppose it is a sword.'

'Honestly! You were absolutely convinced it was a sword yesterday. You went on and on about it.'

'I've changed my mind,' said Mick flatly. The truth was that Mick still did think it was a sword but he didn't want to be disappointed if the test that Mr Ferris was arranging turned out to prove the sword to be worthless rusting metal. Mick switched on the detector and began to walk slowly round the edge of the pond. It wasn't long before the machine started whining and Mick bent down and picked up a fisherman's weight.

'That's not much use,' said Simon, looking at it. 'There haven't been any fish in this pond for ages. There are only those ducks and a few flies.'

'Maybe somebody was fishing for ducks?' suggested Mick. 'At least I suppose you couldn't fish for ducks, you'd have to duck for them.'

'Not very funny,' said Simon. 'Go on.' Mick went on round the pond until the detector started whining once more. He bent down, grubbing around with his fingers in the mud at the pond's edge.

'What is it this time?' asked Simon.

'Don't know. Must be under the mud. Here, you can do the digging. Mum will kill me if I go home filthy.'

Simon began to wrench at the mud with his hands and soon got himself covered. 'You ought to be doing the digging. Get yourself in practice for the garden,' said Simon.

'Ha ha. Not very funny. Have you found it?'

'I can feel something, but it's large and heavy.' Simon plunged his hands deeper and pulled and tugged. Mick joined him. Whatever it was they had found it seemed well and truly stuck in the mud. They pulled harder and all at once there was a slurping gloop from the mud. The object lifted out and the boys lost their footing and sat back heavily in all the disturbed black mud. Mick hastily scrambled to his feet, brushing the mud from his trousers and spreading it even further over his clothing as he did so.

'My mum will kill me!' he groaned.

'I'll arrange the funeral,' said Simon helpfully. 'What sort of flowers would you like?'

'It's not funny,' Mick said quickly. 'What did we pull out anyway?' They looked at the long, sloppy piece of metal. 'Looks like a chain,' Mick said. Simon traced one end of the chain into the lake and the other into the long grass, away from the thick mud.

'It is a long chain. Look, it comes through the grass and stops here. It's fastened to a big ring set in concrete.' Mick came over and eyed the ring and the chain thoughtfully.

'What do you think is on the other end?' asked Simon.

'Don't know. Maybe a sunken boat. You know, a rowing boat or something.'

'Let's pull it up and see.'

The boys grabbed the dirty, wet chain with both hands and began to haul on it. Whatever was on the other end seemed firmly stuck at first. The boys dug their feet further into the grass and pulled even harder. The chain began to move. It gave a quick movement first and then the boys dragged it in, hand over hand, and at last a large round object was hauled out of the lake and lay dripping at their feet.

'What is it?' Simon asked. They stared at it, quite puzzled.

'I'm not sure. I'll tell you what it reminds me of though,' said Mick in a voice that sounded just a shade anxious. 'It looks like a gigantic bath-plug.'

Simon stared at his friend and his face went white. Then they looked with horror at the pond. Sure enough they could already see a rim of scum round the edge where the water had gone down. A tiny stream of bubbles was rising to the surface in the pond's centre.

'It's going down!' cried Simon. 'We've pulled the plug out! Do something!'

'What do you expect me to do? Dive in and put the plug back? How were we to know this pond had a plug in it. Whoever heard of a pond with a plug in? It's daft.'

By now the pond was half empty and the little group of ducks were swimming round faster and faster, quacking in a most disturbed fashion. Mick and Simon wanted to run as far away as they could but at the same time they were hypnotised by the rapidly disappearing water. Bit by bit the bottom of the pond was revealed, until there was just a wet, muddy hollow with a lot of weed draped across it. The ducks carried on going round just as if the water was still there. Their slapping feet made tracks round and round the edge.

Mick spoke quietly to himself. 'How to get rid of a pond,' he said. 'In one easy lesson. On our programme today two expert pond-destroyers, Mick Shaw and Simon Crane, will show you how to remove a pond.'

'Pull the plug out,' whispered Simon. 'We'd better go.'

'We'd better run,' said Mick, and they set off down the hill. It wasn't until Mick reached home and was in the kitchen that he remembered how filthy he was. By that time it was too late because Mum had already seen. She just about killed him, but not quite.

5

It was only a short time after Simon and Mick had pulled the plug from the pond that they saw a police car travel slowly up the hill. Two policemen emerged and wandered over to the pond, where they spent some time before getting back into the car and returning down the hill. Then again, later on, a fire engine made its way up. This gathered a lot of onlookers and Mick and Simon joined them, safe in the knowledge that nobody knew who had caused the sudden disappearance of the pond.

The firemen pulled on great thigh-length wading boots and sloshed their way across the muddy exposed pond bottom, carrying the giant plug. The ducks were still there, only now they were sitting dismally on a pile of drying waterweed and emitting some very melancholy quacks every few minutes.

Having replaced the plug, the firemen rigged up a hose to their water-tanker and within half an hour the pond was back to normal. The boys were delighted. They had never meant to cause any damage and had been sorry to see how downhearted the ducks were. Now everything was fine. The ducks quacked so cheerfully you would have thought Christmas had come eight months early.

However, Mick and Simon had been a little scared and they decided to give up hunting for

FIRE

treasure with the metal-detector for the time being.

'We're hardly likely to find anything anyway,' Simon pointed out.

'True, but that doesn't help me in my present time of economic difficulty.'

'What does that mean?' asked Simon. 'You watch too much television. Sometimes I can't understand a word you say.'

'It means I still haven't got any money. In fact I still owe 14p.'

'Well go and dig your Mum's garden,' said Simon.

But Mick still wasn't keen on that idea. There was too much hard work involved in it. There was a fast approaching roar and a motorcycle burned up the road and rapidly disappeared.

'That was probably Andy,' said Simon.

'Who's Andy?'

'He's my sister's boyfriend – you know, the one with the giant earrings.'

'Who, Andy? With giant earrings?' asked Mick incredulously.

'Don't be daft. My sister. Andy's a courier. He has to whizz about on a motor bike all day long carrying messages and things for customers.'

Mick was astounded. 'You mean he gets paid for riding about on a motor bike all day long?' Simon nodded. Mick murmured softly. 'And my Mum offers me two pounds to dig the garden. I tell you

Simon, it's . . .'

'Slave labour,' interrupted his friend. 'Yes, you've told me before.'

'Well, if your sister's boyfriend Andy can do it, I don't see why I shouldn't.'

'Shouldn't what?'

'Be a courier and take messages for people and charge them money for it.'

Simon sat down on a wall and considered Mick's idea. 'What about the motorbike?' he asked eventually. 'You haven't got a motorbike and you couldn't ride one even if you did have.'

'I've got a bike.'

Simon had to admit he was impressed. It sounded quite reasonable to him. Mick said that he would start straight away, and he hurried home to prepare everything.

It was quite true that Mick had a bike, but he did not often use it and the reason for that was quite simple. The bike was old and Mick did not feel too happy riding it, especially when he was faced with an upward-sloping hill. Since Mick lived in an area where there were quite a large number of hills he didn't often ride the bike, and since Mick did not often ride the bike Mick's parents saw little point in replacing it with a new one.

So Mick went to the shed and pulled the bike out. He also pulled out an old stair-carpet, the grass box for the lawn mower, and two garden chairs, all of which had been sitting on top of the bicycle. Mrs Shaw called out from an upstairs window.

'Are you going to put all those things back?'

'Of course!' How could Mick's mum doubt him?

'When?'

'Next year,' muttered Mick to himself. 'Now,' he shouted. Mum closed the window. Mick wearily replaced all the articles in the shed. 'I might just as

well have lived in Roman times,' he thought. 'I'm a slave, a child slave.'

Having got everything else back in the shed Mick propped his bike against the house wall and checked it over. It was impossible to tell what colour the bike had originally been because it was now so encrusted with dirt and grease and rust. Mick kicked the frame and grunted. Flakes of rust trickled onto the ground. Certainly it was a bike. It had two wheels, one at each end. It even had a saddle, although most of the leather had peeled off and there was just a row of small springs to sit on. It had handlebars too, crooked and dented and covered in black tape that was peeling off in long strips. Some of the spokes were missing from each wheel. It hardly looked like a world speed-record breaker. At least the tyres were hard.

The next step was to make out a notice. Mick wrote out a large sign that said:

MICK SHAW –
LIGHTNING MESSAGE SERVICE

He cut this to the shape of the bicycle frame and then pinched Mum's sellotape and fixed the sign on to the bike. He was all set up and ready to go. The only problem was where he was going to get his customers from. Mick wheeled his bike out onto the street, parked it outside a house and walked up the path. He knocked on the door and after a while a lady with blue hair came to the door. It was Mrs Evans.

'Oh, hello Mick, what can I do for you?' Mick wondered why it was that ladies had their hair turned blue. He had seen quite a few like it. Maybe they were colour-blind, or maybe they were part of a secret society that recognised each other by their blue hair. It could be that Mrs Evans was a secret agent for Colonel Garst.

'Yes Mick?' repeated Mrs Evans, patting her hair because she had become unnerved by Mick's constant staring at it. Mick cleared his throat.

'Do you need any messages taken Mrs Evans?' Mick was suddenly struck by a terrible thought. Supposing Mrs Evans was a spy working for Colonel Garst and she asked Mick to take one of her secret messages for her? That would make him a traitor to his country. He could be flung into prison for that. He stepped down from the porch.

'What do you mean?' asked Mrs Evans. 'What sort of messages?'

'I'm a messenger service,' said Mick. 'Lightning delivery by hand of any messages in this area.'

'Oh, I see.' Mrs Evans gave a smile. 'And I suppose you have to be paid for this special service?' she enquired. Mick reddened.

'Just a token charge.'

'All right. Actually there is something you can do for me. I've got a little parcel for my sister and I'd like her to have it now but I don't really want to go all that way at the moment. She lives in Crown Road, number 3.'

'Crown Road,' Mick repeated. 'Yes, I know, that's up by the football field.'

Mrs Evans fetched the parcel and handed it to Mick with two tenpenny pieces. Mick was well pleased. He was getting off to a good start. It didn't take him long to pedal over to Crown Road and deliver the parcel. He had rather a shock when Mrs Evans' sister opened the door. She had blue hair too and for a moment Mick was convinced that he had just delivered some deadly secret information to her on behalf of Colonel Garst.

'Oh good,' said the sister. 'This will be the gardening gloves she promised to bring over. I must say I think that's a very clever idea of yours – having a messenger service.' Mick smiled and hurried back to his own road. As he neared Simon's house there was a hiss and it suddenly felt as if he were riding a bike with square wheels. The back tyre had a puncture. Mick got off and wheeled the bike over to Simon's.

'What's that!' cried Simon. 'Which museum did that come from?'

'Listen. It might not look good but it does me fine. This bike has just earned me twenty pence,' and Mick explained about his messenger service, and then pointed out the puncture.

Simon willingly set to and helped Mick mend it, though it took about half an hour. Mrs Crane came out and asked them what they were doing. Mick had to explain all over again.

'You can take a message for me when you've finished doing that puncture,' she said. 'Our telephone's out of order at the moment so I could do with a messenger.' Mrs Crane turned to Simon. 'It's a pity *you* didn't think of a good idea like that.' Mick just grinned while Simon bit his lip to stop himself saying something rude.

'Can you go to that glass and mirror shop in the High Street, Mick? Do you know the one I mean?' Mick nodded.

'Well, I need a piece of glass. One of our window panes is cracked and Simon's dad said that if I order it today he can collect it on the way home from work.

Just tell them at the shop I want some window glass, three by two. Those are the measurements, three by two. Do you want me to write them down?'

'I can remember that easily,' said Mick. 'Three by two window glass and Mr Crane will collect it this afternoon.'

'Well done. Now, how much do I owe you?'

'Mrs Evans gave me 20p,' Mick said.

'Well I'll give you thirty because there's a big hill on the way, isn't there.'

Simon jumped up and kicked over the bowl of water they had been using to trace Mick's puncture. It soaked his feet. 'That isn't fair!' cried Simon. 'It's only uphill on the way there. It's downhill on the way back.'

'Thirty pence,' repeated Mrs Crane firmly, and she fetched her bag. 'You'd better go and change your shoes and socks,' she told Simon.

Mick pedalled off furiously to the High Street. His spirits were soaring as he felt a whole fifty pence bouncing up and down in his left-hand pocket. At this rate he'd be rich in no time. If he could take five messages in the morning and five in the afternoon that was about two pounds every day. In a week he'd have fourteen pounds and in a month he'd have . . . A car hooted at him as he swerved dreamily across the road. Well, in a month he'd have a lot of money of course.

Mick came to the hill. It was horribly long and

steep. He pedalled as far as he could and then gave up, dismounted, and pushed his bike the rest of the way. He had to scurry across the road to the other side when he suddenly noticed one of Colonel Garst's blue haired secret agents coming straight towards him. Luckily she didn't notice. Mick waited until she had safely passed and then lobbed two hand-grenades after her and blew her sky-high. He had to throw himself to the ground to avoid the blast and his bike toppled over with a rusty clatter.

'Do you mind?' said a high, stern voice. It was a posh-looking lady with a dachshund trotting at her heels. 'That wretched bike almost fell on Tootsie. It gave her a terrible fright. What on earth were you doing?'

Mick dragged himself to his feet and brushed the dust from his sleeves. 'Oh, I was just eliminating

one of the world's most fiendish secret agents.' he answered casually, getting onto his bike.

'I beg your pardon?'

'I was just blowing that old lady up,' said Mick, and before the posh lady or dachshund could say anything he rode off, leaving them both quite bewildered.

When he reached the glaziers Mick left his bike outside and marched straight in.

'Mrs Crane would like a piece of window glass,' he said to the ginger-haired and highly freckled glass-cutter.

'Oh yes, I know. She's been in before. What size does she want young lad?'

'She said three by two,' answered Mick firmly. The man grinned and gave a little laugh.

'Oho. She said three by two did she?' Mick nodded. 'She didn't happen to tell you three what by two what, did she? Did she say three inches or three feet, or three metres or three centimetres? We use all of those at the moment.'

Mick was thunderstruck. Three by two what? It was very confusing.

'You're not sure are you? Let's give her a ring.'

'The 'phone doesn't work,' said Mick. 'That's why she sent me.' His brain was whirring away rapidly. Three by two, but what? He remembered having heard Mr Crane often talking about metres and things so maybe it was that.

'I think it's metres.' he said.

'That would be a pretty big pane of glass. Enormous in fact,' said the freckle-faced man. This convinced Mick he was right, because Mr and Mrs Crane had a modern house with enormous windows at the front and the back. He was sure the glass was for one of those.

The glazier carefully measured out the glass and put it to one side.

'Mr Crane will collect it on his way home from work,' said Mick.

'I don't think so. He'll never get this in his car. Don't worry, we'll deliver it. Won't cost them any extra. We'll bring it over later this afternoon.'

Mick got back on his bike and went to Simon's. At least the hill went down this time. He saw the blue-haired spy on the way too so he launched six bicycle-mounted torpedoes at her and she sank without a trace in a shark-infested pavement. That was another of Colonel Garst's agents successfully dealt with.

Mrs Crane was pleased at Mick's promptness and he was invited to tea. So when Mr Crane came in from work Mick was sitting at their kitchen table with his friend. Mr Crane was puzzled. There had been no glass at the glaziers. The assistant had told him it was on the delivery van. Why should they want to deliver it. It was only three by two. Mick had an unpleasant feeling in his stomach.

The doorbell rang. It was the glazier with a piece of glass three metres by two metres. Mr Crane took one look at it and almost died laughing.

'What do we want that for?' he cried. 'All I've

got to replace is a cracked pane in the kitchen door, three feet by two feet.' Mr Crane looked at his wife. Mrs Crane looked at Mick. He pushed his pudding to one side.

'I don't think I'm very hungry today,' he said. He pulled another grenade from his pocket and blew himself up.

6

Luckily the mistake over the glass was easily sorted out. Mick couldn't really be blamed for the error, especially as Mrs Crane quickly pointed out that she had told Mick three by two and hadn't given him further instructions. Mr Crane told his wife off instead.

When Mick went home after tea on his rusty bike he got a second puncture. He quickly decided that if he was going to get punctures every five minutes and create havoc by giving wrong messages he had better give up his lightning messenger service before it was too late. He altered his list.

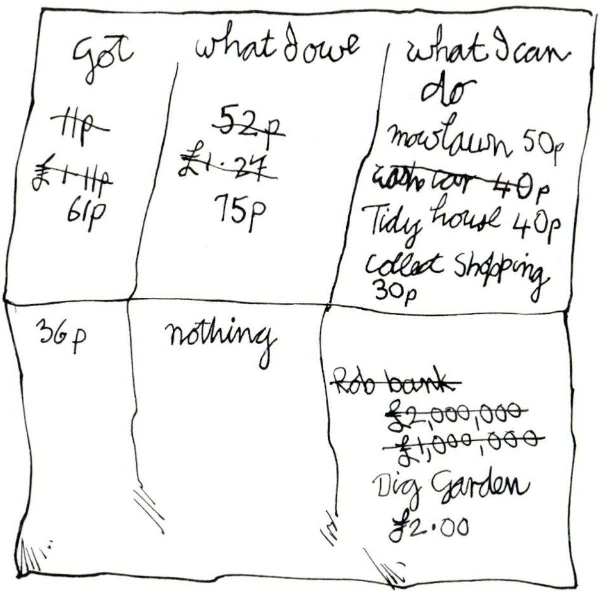

It made quite an impressive statement. No debts, 36p in his pocket and the prospect of earning a further two pounds if he wanted to break his back digging the garden. The very idea gave him backache. If he did that, he'd have to spend his £2.36 on medicine from the chemist. In fact he'd probably end up in hospital, flat on his back, paralysed for weeks. He wouldn't be able to eat or drink. The doctors would have to invent an automatic Mick's mouth opener that opened his mouth every five minutes and shoved in some chocolate or some peanuts.

'Mick? Mick, are you day-dreaming again?' It was Dad. 'Tell me, have you got that 75p you owe me?' Mick handed the money over.

'It's robbery,' he murmured.

'Nonsense. You're the one that put the oil all over the car. Why don't you do something that won't get you into trouble. Mow the lawn perhaps?'

Mick began to wonder why Mum and Dad kept suggesting that he mowed the lawn. Perhaps it was because they didn't want to do it themselves.

'I can't at the moment,' he said.

'Why ever not?'

'Well, I'm allergic to lawnmowers. Every time I go near a lawnmower, I get a dreadful fit of coughing and I can hardly breathe. I go all dizzy and my legs wobble and my face comes up in bright green spots and . . .'

'Mick! You're making things up again. If you spent less time day-dreaming and more getting on and doing things you wouldn't be so overweight.' Mr Shaw was getting a bit cross.

'I'm not overweight!' Mick protested. 'This is protection against the time I'm lost in a desert.'

'There you go again, dreaming,' said Mr Shaw. 'When are you ever likely to get lost in a desert?' There was a long silence while Mick thought of an answer. At last he spoke.

'It's very unlikely,' he admitted, and hastily added, 'but all the same I ought to be prepared.' Mr Shaw managed to laugh.

'Listen Mick, I'll tell you what I'll do. I know you're desperate for money at the moment so I'll do a deal with you. If you can lose three pounds of weight over the next week, I'll give you 50p for every pound you lose. That's £1.50!'

Mick looked carefully at his father. 'You want me to lose some weight? This is a sort of sponsored weight-loss?' It was a long way from Mick's idea of a sponsored feast, but £1.50 was a lot of money.

'Fifty pence for every pound you lose,' Dad repeated. 'How about it?'

'When do I start?'

'Right now, of course. There's no time like the present.'

'All right,' said Mick. 'I'll do it.' Dad smiled and went downstairs to watch television.

Mick lay back on his bed and thought. Surely he wouldn't have to give up much to lose three pounds of weight? If he missed out having his bite of supper just before he went to sleep, he would probably lose pounds and pounds in no time at all. By the time a few days had passed Mum would have to buy him new sets of extra-slim clothes because his old stuff would be far too big. Simon wouldn't be able to recognise him. Mick was quite taken by the idea.

When his bed-time came round, Mick was about to sit down at the kitchen table for a quick slice of bread and apricot jam when Dad rushed in, waving a newspaper.

'What are you doing? Have you forgotten your

sponsored diet?' Mick suddenly remembered. He sighed and pushed the plate to one side, got up slowly and went to bed. After he had gone Mr Shaw turned to his wife and winked.

'I think this will really work, you know. Mick needs to lose a bit of weight.'

'He's not terribly overweight. He's just a big boy for his age,' defended Mum. 'As he gets older he's bound to lose a lot of that excess weight.'

'I don't like to see him podgy,' frowned Dad. 'He can earn some money and lose weight at the same time. It's an excellent idea.'

'Let's wait and see,' Mum said. 'I'm not sure it will work.' She glanced at the slice of bread and jam that Mick had left behind on the table. Dad smiled at her and ate it himself.

At about half past two in the morning Mick woke up. He had just had a terrible dream. First of all he was in a rowing boat all by himself, rowing madly across a stormy sea towards an island made of sponge cake and chocolate icing. Every time he tried to land his little boat on the island it disappeared beneath the waves and came bobbing up somewhere else. At last he managed to run his boat up the spongy beach but as soon as he jumped out and landed on the delicious cake it turned to burning sand. The rowing boat vanished and Mick realised with horror that he was now in the middle of the Sahara Desert.

Glaring sand stretched to the horizon in every direction. He began to walk and after he had trudged for hours he came across a sign that said *Sahara Café – 100 metres on right*. Mick hurried on and saw the cafe ahead of him. He crawled on his knees up to the counter and there was Simon serving behind the counter and grinning at Mick like a deranged monkey.

Mick asked for a giant ice-cream with crushed walnuts, chocolate sauce and fresh strawberries. Simon offered him an old sock. The Sahara Café suddenly vanished and Mick woke up trembling,

with an awful stomach ache. He sat up and wiped his sweating brow. He knew what that hollow rumble in his stomach meant. It meant he was hungry. He glanced at the clock. Twenty to three. It was still pitch dark outside.

Mick sat up in bed listening to the night sounds. He could hear his clock ticking steadily and the funny little creaks and squeaks that always come from a house at night. Simon had once spent the night at Mick's and had asked Mick what all the creaky noises were. Mick had explained that at night their house usually went for walks down the road and back again while everyone was asleep. The problem was that Simon had believed him and wanted to go home, so Mick told him he was only joking.

It was no good, Mick thought. He would have to go downstairs to the kitchen and get some food. Dad wouldn't know and anyway it wouldn't matter. Mick carefully got out of bed and slipped on his dressing gown and slippers. He tip-toed across to the door and crept down the stairs, being very careful to avoid the creaky steps. At the bottom he waited to see if Mum or Dad came hurrying out to see what was going on, but nothing happened so Mick went straight into the kitchen and switched on the light. He peered round at the cupboards and shelves, rubbing his hands together. Now, what was he going to have for his midnight feast?

First of all he got out the bread and the apricot jam and the strawberry jam and the chocolate spread and the golden syrup. He carefully cut four slices of bread and spread one slice with each. He sat down on a kitchen chair and slowly munched his way through the four slices. A smile spread across his face. That felt a bit better. Now, what could he have next? He fetched the breakfast cereal and poured himself a bowl of cereal with milk and sugar. Halfway through eating it he remembered that Mum had bought a packet of digestive biscuits and put them at the top of the cupboard, so he pulled his chair over to the cupboard and stood on it and reached up onto the back shelf to fetch the biscuits.

Unfortunately the biscuits had been pushed right to the rear of the cupboard and Mick couldn't actually see what he was doing, so he had to grope around with his fingers. Suddenly there was a horrible snap and an excruciating pain leapt up one finger as it got caught in a mouse-trap. Mick gave a high-pitched scream and toppled back from the chair and fell across one end of the kitchen table.

The other end of the table was launched into the air like a see-saw and the bottle of milk and cereal bowl were catapulted halfway across the room, together with two jam-pots, the tub of chocolate and the syrup jar. They landed with a horrible mixture of breaking glass and slapping oozy messes. Glass shattered and spread across the floor. The jams and syrup and chocolate slowly expanded in sticky puddles. Mick lay across the table with an expression of great anguish fixed on his face and the mousetrap dangling from one finger.

Heavy footsteps on the stairs announced the arrival of Mum and Dad. Dad came rushing into the kitchen and stepped straight into the sticky mess of jam and syrup. He was waving a large stick in one hand and shouting at the top of his voice.

'Police! Police! This is the police!' He seemed to think that the kitchen was full of burglars. When he saw Mick lying across the table with a mouse trap on one finger he suddenly stopped shouting altogether and for several moments he couldn't think of a word to say. Mum stood quietly at the kitchen door looking first at her husband and then at her son and then back at her husband. At last Mr Shaw found his tongue.

'Mick? Mick! What's going on?' Mr Shaw tried to make his way to the table but his slippers stuck to the jam and he couldn't move.

Mick looked up at his father and gave a sort of strange shrug of his shoulders. 'All I wanted was a large ice-cream with walnut and and chocolate sauce and fresh strawberries.'

'What? What are you talking about?'

Mick shook his head. 'I don't know Dad. Something bit my finger and suddenly it seemed as if World War Three had started.'

'But what's been going on!' cried Dad. 'This room looks as if a bomb's just fallen on it. And what's that mousetrap doing on your finger?'

'It hurts Dad,' said Mick. He really was feeling bad.

Mrs Shaw hurried over to her son, carefully avoiding the pools of jam and the broken glass. She quietly removed the mousetrap from Mick's finger and examined it. It was badly bruised and rather swollen.

'I'll rub some cream on it,' she said. Mick looked at it with great interest. He was wondering what a cat would have said if it had found Mick caught in a mousetrap instead of a real mouse.

Dad didn't say any more about the mess. Mick was put back to bed and he soon fell into a dreamless sleep, while Mum and Dad cleared up downstairs.

'That's the end of Mick losing weight,' said Dad. 'Just look at the mess he's made.' Mum kept quiet. She had thought all along that Mick would not keep to his diet.

The following morning there was a lot of talking and arguing. Mick kept pointing out that he needed food. Dad kept saying he would have to pay for the jam and the syrup and everything.

'Food costs money and money doesn't grow on trees,' said Dad several times. 'You've wasted about two pounds worth of food there so you can give your mother one pound towards replacements.'

'A pound!' cried Mick. His face dropped. 'A whole pound! But that's all the money I've earned and my pocket money and I shall still owe 4p after that!'

Dad got up and stood there angrily. 'I didn't break everything!' he said noisily. 'I didn't get up in the middle of the night and break jam pots all over the kitchen floor and spill milk everywhere and get my fingers caught in mousetraps. You've wasted far more than two pounds. You're jolly lucky I haven't told you to pay for everything.' Dad stalked out of the room and left Mick with his head hanging. He was quite broken. Mum tried to cheer him up.

'You can always dig the garden,' she said.

'Why is it I always owe money?' he asked his mother. 'It doesn't matter how much money I earn,

I always seem to end up owing more than I've earned.'

He stared dolefully at the kitchen table. Mum sat down opposite.

'I don't understand why you want all this money in the first place,' she said.

'I need it,' said Mick.

'But what for? What are you going to do with it?'

Mick racked his brains. What did he need all the money for?

'Everybody needs money,' said Mick. 'Look at Dad. He always needs money.'

'Yes, but Dad pays for the house and the food and the electricity and so on. You don't have to pay for any of those.'

'I have to pay for all the jam and syrup,' Mick said darkly.

'Well, if you desperately need money I suggest you dig the garden.'

Mick frowned. Dig the garden. It was the only course open to him. He stood up and went to the kitchen window and stared out over the garden to the bottom where Mum wanted to put a vegetable patch.

'You know what this is?' he muttered quietly. 'It's . . .'

'Slave labour,' Mum said for him. 'I know. Go on, get out there and start digging, slave.'

7

A further disappointment for Mick came when the postman arrived. There was a letter for him. It was quite unusual for Mick to receive any post and he was naturally anxious to see what it could be. Even his Mum and Dad came and waited behind his shoulder. They couldn't think what it was either. The letter was from Mr Ferris at the Museum.

Dear Mick,
The results of the tests on your object have just come back to me. I'm sorry to say that it is not a sword, nor anything like a sword. Apparently it is part of some farm machinery and it dates from about 1900. Unfortunately this also means that it is worthless so you will not be receiving £1 000 either. Don't be too disappointed – keep up the searching. One day you may find something that is really worthwhile.

Yours sincerely,
R.D. Ferris.

Mick's dad frowned as he read. 'What's all this about a sword and £1 000, Mick?' Mick told them about the metal-detector and Mr Ferris. He left out the bit concerning Colonel Garst disguised as a horse and the explosive grass.

Mum thought the story was quite amusing. Dad started to say something about 'you shouldn't waste other people's time like that.' Mum stopped him. 'I think it was clever of Mick to think of finding out what it was. After all, if the thing was so heavily covered with rust, it could have been a sword.' Mick smiled at his mum gratefully and she winked at him. Dad agreed begrudgingly that perhaps Mick had done the right thing.

Mick read through the letter once more and then slowly tore it up and put it in the bin. That meant no £1 000 and that in turn meant that he would have to forget about buying himself a 200mph go-kart. The idea of the go-kart had only occurred a couple of days previously. It came from when he was doing the Lightning Messenger Service and having to push his bike up hills. At the time, he had this brilliant thought that what he needed was a go-kart. Then he'd be able to scorch around the streets at 200mph, delivering messages at high speed and earning fantastic sums of money. When he had given up the idea of the messenger service he still thought he could do with a go-kart. Mick could just picture himself tearing up his road on the way to Simon's house with flames leaping from his exhaust pipes and the tyres leaving screeching black slip-marks round all the corners.

Mick sighed. Perhaps it was a good thing after all. He didn't suppose the police would be too impressed by a ten-year old maniac on a go-kart.

'What are you going to do now?' Mum asked.

'Where's the spade?' Mick asked.

'Are you going to dig my vegetable patch?'

'I haven't got much choice, have I?' answered Mick dully. Mum smiled and patted his back.

'Never mind. Just think, once you've finished you'll have earned two whole pounds.'

'By the time I've finished that digging,' groaned Mick, 'I shall be half-dead. In fact you may as well order my coffin for me now and while I'm out there digging the vegetable patch I'll dig my own grave and you can put the coffin in the bottom and when I finish the digging I shall just collapse with exhaustion and topple into the coffin. All you'll have to do is put the lid on. Tell Simon he can have all my toys after I'm gone, won't you?'

Mick collected the spade and trailed off down the garden path.

The ground was difficult to dig because it had never been dug before and was covered with thick grass. Mick's parents could not remember there ever having been a vegetable patch on that bit of ground, not even when they bought the house, long before Mick was born.

He had to clear the grass off the top first. That was an awkward job in itself. All the roots were tangled up together. Mick found the best way was to slide the spade beneath the turf to cut the roots and then roll the grass back. That left the bare earth ready for digging. Mick began to wish he had a few sticks of dynamite that he could plant like potatoes in the ground. Then he could just blow up the mud and leave everything nice and ready for planting vegetables. As he began to thrust his spade into the ground Mick could just picture himself coming out of a dive in his Phantom jet. There was a crackle of messages on his intercom:

'Mum to Mick. Mum to Mick, can you hear me?'

'I can hear you Mum, coming out of sighting dive now, flying at 250 metres, speed 2500km/h. Ready to drop bombs, Roger and out.' Mick flipped the jet over and flew upside down and then flipped back to normal. The house and garden shot into view. The jets whined furiously behind his head and he pulled the bomb release. Pam! Pam! Pam! Pam!

Four bombs scored direct hits on the garden as Mick put the jet into a screaming climb. He looked back over his shoulder, saw the smoking, perfect shape of a vegetable garden on the lawn and did a victory roll.

At that moment Mick's spade struck something with a dull thud and Mick's daydream vanished. He bent down to see what he had hit. He pushed aside the crumbly earth with his hands and groaned. It was a large flattish piece of rusty metal. Oh well, at least it couldn't be a sword. Mick tried to get a grip on the metal but wherever his fingers probed he just felt the same slightly rounded flat surface. He pushed the spade in around it and tried to lever the object out, but it wouldn't budge. Mick then tried to dig right round the thing, but he then discovered that it was quite large.

What was it? What could be so large, made of metal, and buried in the back of their garden?

Was it a metal coffin, housing Dracula? Or perhaps a crashed Martian space-craft, an unexploded bomb, or one of those satellites that sometimes fell out of the sky. Mick dug a bit further round the object and brushed away the mud and dirt that caked the outside. He now revealed part of a long, cylindrical thing. Mick could not see either end of it. They were both firmly buried in the earth. It was obvious that Mick would never be able to move it by himself. He flung down the spade happily because he couldn't dig the garden until the object was removed. He went up to the kitchen. Mum wasn't there. She and Dad had both gone up to the High Street to get some shopping, so Mick went round to Simon's house.

'Hello Moneybags,' was Simon's greeting. 'What are you up to?'

Mick explained about the garden and the buried object.

'Perhaps it's a bomb?' suggested Simon.

'What would a bomb be doing in our garden?' asked Mick. 'Unless of course Colonel Garst is trying to blow me up.'

'Well what do you think it is?' asked Simon.

'I don't know. Come and see it for yourself. You may be able to help me move it.'

Simon went over to the garden with Mick and the two boys stood over the buried object and peered at it. They were quite bewildered.

'Are you sure it's not a buried car?' said Simon.

'I mean, you remember that tea-caddy and the dead bird? Maybe somebody's buried their old car in your garden.'

'Ha ha. Look, just get this fork and we'll try and lever it out.'

Mick and Simon spent a quarter of an hour digging and straining but they could not make the object move a fraction. All they did was reveal a bit more of the surface. They were standing there, sweating and panting, when Mr Shaw wandered down to see them.

'Hello, have you given up all ready Mick?'

'I'm stuck because of this thing,' said Mick, pointing at the buried object. Dad came closer and stared down at it.

'What is it?' he asked. The boys shook their heads and Mick shrugged.

Dad bent down and rubbed away some mud and rust. He began to mutter to himself under his breath. Then he turned very slowly to Simon and Mick and spoke in a curiously quiet voice.

'You two go up to the house for a moment, will you?'

'Why Dad?' asked Mick, puzzled.

'Do as you're told.' His voice was so harsh that Mick and Simon obeyed instantly.

About two minutes later, Dad followed them up to the house. He went at once to the telephone. Mick was surprised to see the telephone shaking in Dad's hand.

'Police please,' said Dad. Mick and Simon sat bolt upright.

'Oh, good morning. I think I've got an unexploded bomb in my back garden . . . yes, a bomb . . . my son was digging a vegetable patch . . . yes it's large, about a metre long, maybe more . . . there's some writing in German on it that you can still just see . . . what? . . . oh yes, of course, we won't go anywhere near it . . .'

Dad gave the address of the house and came slowly into the front room and sat down. He looked at Mrs Shaw who was standing in the doorway with an expression of horror frozen on her face. Her lips moved as if she were trying to say something but no sound came out.

'Is it really a bomb, Dad?' asked Mick.

"Let's wait and see.'

'But how did it get there?' Mick couldn't believe it had really happened.

'If it is a bomb it must have been dropped in the last war, I suppose,' Dad replied.

'But people can't go leaving bombs lying about!' said Simon. 'Suppose it blows up!'

'Oh don't say that, Simon,' said Mrs Shaw hurriedly.

Simon looked away from her frightened face and stared at his knees. Mick was silent.

The wail of a distant police car siren floated over the houses, getting steadily closer. Mr Shaw got to his feet, glanced at his wife and went out to meet the new arrivals. There was a short squeal of brakes and doors slammed. Mick felt as if he were in the middle of a movie and everything was plotted out carefully. The snatches of tense conversation, the strained faces. . . .

He stood up and went over to the big window where Mum was already staring out. They could see Mr Shaw and four policemen bending over the object Mick had unearthed. They saw their lips moving as they spoke to each other, but not a word pierced the clear glass of the window. Then Dad came back up the path with one of the policemen.

The policeman went straight to the telephone

but Dad came into the back room and said, quite simply, 'We've got to get out. It's a bomb. We've got to get out – move out of the house.' He repeated it again as if he couldn't quite believe it all. Then he added, 'The police think that Mick may have activated the timing device when he disturbed it.'

Mrs Shaw almost screamed but managed to get a hand over her mouth in time. She gave her head a funny little shake, shut her eyes for just a moment and when she opened them she was quite sensible again.

'You two boys go to Simon's house. Mrs Crane won't mind.'

'You go with them,' said Mr Shaw. For a second they all looked at each other, wondering what Mr Shaw was going to do. After all, they all had to go, even Mr Shaw. It was strange. Mr Shaw shrugged. 'I'd better come too,' he murmured helplessly.

Round at the Crane's house things were even stranger. Everybody sat stiff and silent, as if they expected an explosion at any moment. Mick could hear a silent ticking deep inside his brain – the slow unwinding of a bomb's timing device.

Another siren wailed away and something rushed past the Crane's house. Mr Shaw turned away from the window and smiled weakly at Mick.

'I don't know how you manage it, Mick. All we asked you to do was dig the garden.'

'I didn't know,' said Mick. 'I wouldn't have

gone anywhere near it if I'd known. You're lucky I'm still here. I could be flying through the air in a million pieces by now . . .'

'Mick!' squeaked Mum. 'Don't say such things! That's horrible.'

'Anyway,' continued Mick. 'There ought to be a reward for finding unexploded bombs.'

Then the silence came back into the room, even heavier than before. It seemed to weigh down upon them so much they ended up with their heads bowed to the floor and not a word was spoken.

The telephone rang and everybody jumped to answer it. Mr Shaw was first and the others watched his face intently. A slow smile began to signal success all round the room, and even before the others had heard the exact details they were leaping up and down laughing and making jokes about bombs. Mick whispered to Simon something about Colonel Garst being foiled yet again.

The Cranes offered everybody tea, but Mr and Mrs Shaw wanted to get back to their own house and see if it really was safe and in one piece, so Mr Crane ran them back in his car. The police and two army officers were still there and Mick took the opportunity to ask if there was any reward for his discovery. Much to his disappointment there was none but when he went down the garden to see where the bomb had been he discovered with great delight that the Bomb Disposal Squad had dug up

almost the whole of the vegetable patch in order to remove the bomb. All the hard work had been done for him. Mick marched back to the house and claimed his two pounds. He couldn't think why he needed the money so much, but he was certain he could think of something. Mick gently patted his stomach. It was time he made serious preparations against being marooned in the Sahara Desert. After all, with bombs in the garden, you never know what might happen next.